How to Protect Your Children Online

Internet Safety Tips for Kids

Written by Madison Owen

Contents

Introduction

Children tend to explore things that they think they are capable of doing. They crave for more things beyond what they can do. For that, they want to know more about the world.

With the new technology of internet, everything would be possible than what their parents think. The task becomes easier by just a few keystrokes in the keyboard and less than 8 seconds the website of their choice is there. For that, what children want to know and needed is already presented in the website.

When children are exposed to the internet, they are also close to new ways in exploring things. There are many things they can do such as searching for their favorite movies, television series, books or latest updates of their favorite shows.

If they think that these things can harm them, they will take advantage of the unlimited availability of information in the internet. There are certain websites that a child can land on that parents may think are safe.

But they do not know that some of them have chat rooms that can be the culprit of danger for a child. Even though some would say that they are not interested with this thing. As what mentioned earlier, a child will be curious beyond what he is capable of.

When he gets bored accessing same things all over, he might try to use the chat room and look for someone he can call an online friend. These people are strangers to them, but when they become open, children might feel comfortable talking to them.

Once they found out how interesting this application, they will seek out more friends that are in the circle of their interests. What they do not know, they are putting their selves on danger if they are not careful of the information they are giving. On the other hand, these people would be like a wolf pretending to offer a friendship but once they see the chance they would grab for the sheep. This so called friendship that the children think they have become more serious that they start to open their life to them and told all things what they felt.

All the emotions and problems they felt will be confined from some strangers they only met online. Thinking that the other person whom they trust can really help them from what they are going through. Far from what they know, this person is only taking advantage of the emotional distress that your child is going through. Your child will be lured from the fake intention of the person is giving such as promises, attention and love over the internet.

As soon as they see that your child is already comfortable with them, they start to introduce the contents of pornography or gambling. As children get to be too curious, they will surely find out more. This will be the start that the strangers will continuously giving them the sexual images and talks on a sexually explicit manner. In short, they are slowly being brainwashed by their so called friends.

Your children will start to show actions of starting to grow up faster than they need aside from their normal life as a child. Sooner that these people think that your children are already ready to move into being friends from another level, they will talk of meeting up in personal.

Once this thing happen, your children will be on the hands of the stranger for a long period of time. That is when parents worry for their child's safety and do whatever to have their child back. People who are doing this over the internet vary on age limits. They are not usually old and some of them are only a little older than your child. They can be good in luring your children, no matter what the age, and that is the parents' problem.

Though others may not on the field of child molester but still they can do harm in your children in other way that parents should always be prepared and aware.

Internet: Child's Library of Information

Accessing information in the old times was never convenient. Long ago, only males are allowed to go to school and achieved a degree in Philosophy or Literature. But as soon as the Middle Ages came, information and knowledge were only in the hands of religious people not until Renaissance came that they were allowed to be seen.

Decades and centuries passed, women were also allowed to go to school. People now are granted with all the available information they want to obtain. The day came that everything changes and made accessing information very easy for everyone.

First, we have these libraries where collections of books were stocked in order. Until we came to databases where all information are stored in a way that we could search through and retrieve without a sweat or passing each aisle in the library. All these databases are made available online and can search them through the internet in just seconds to minute of researching. It is the internet that made the revolutionary step on ways to access the knowledge and given the people around the globe a chance to expand the knowledge beyond what they learned.

This becomes an advantage for children who are studying in accessing information that could help them in their projects and homework. But internet need is very helpful if used in the right way. It is also their means of sharing their knowledge on the field of their expertise from people in their same circle of interests. Through internet, they can easily help out people who are seeking knowledge from an expert. This is true to some children who wanted to learn new things and seek answers from a true expert. We as parents have to know the advantages and disadvantages of internet in our child. The vast information that online contains may be right or wrongly used. As parents we have to know what will be right and wrong for our children. This is not only for them to be aware but also for us that internet is either educational or destruction.

Advantages of Internet in a Child's Life

Here are the advantages of internet as our way to access knowledge in a super express way:

- Information and knowledge are freely given to some specific sites. One of the latest trends for children to search for information are the online free encyclopedia such as Wikipedia that allows experts to post their knowledge of expertise that would be available for everyone to access like a hardbound encyclopedia. There are also other sites that have specific topics and categories of their contents such as science, technology, clothes or fashion. Everything you need is just a few keystrokes away.

- Even though there are certain sites that are not free but there are online merchant sites that offer books or other information that cannot be found on free sites. For example the Amazon and Barnes offer electronic books that children can download and read on their computer than picking up a real heavy book in the library.

- Knowledge is not just presented through text but is also available in different media. It will depend on the users want and learning capabilities. A person who is more visual can watch video, read e-books or pamphlets to obtain the information he or she wants. If a person is more on audio learning, there are many audio media containing information that he can listen to. The way internet presented knowledge in a flexible and versatile manner allows people to gain more learning on the format they want and comfortable with.

These advantages of internet make children's learning without hard ship. These make their time in researching easier for their school projects and home works through retrieving information online.

They can also buy whatever books those are not available in their local libraries. Learning is not difficult for them. Internet had already made it possible for them.

There are many expert people on different fields that can assist the learning of the children. This makes easier than walking through aisle per aisle to look for the books they will be a need on their education.

Disadvantages of Internet in a Child's Life

However, not all will be on the good side. To make things balance, internet has also its own risks. We as parents are caught between the dilemmas how and when internet will be good or bad.

There are thousands of students and children benefited from the knowledge that internet offered them. But on the bad side, it becomes the source of prey to hunt for innocent lambs that are potential victims.

There will be many online thieves and threats hunting information such as credit card or bank account information, phishing or much worse child molesting.

Because of living in this modern time, there will be young children or teenagers whose mindsets are open for the cultural changes that have been occurring and can cope up with this kind of contents.

But there are still those who remain innocents from all the changes and might be the more potential victims if caught up on the mess.

Moreover, here are other disadvantages that internet can have in your children if they are constantly relying on the internet:

- Because information is very easy to access, your children will be encouraged not to read anymore the researches they must conduct and just copy and paste the information. This will make their effort easier on projects and homework. In short, it makes your child lazy from learning his lessons and can lead into plagiarism by their teachers.

- We may also want to be aware that not all contents put online are true. Some of the contents are not edited when there will be changes. As a result, there will be schools that will require the banning of usage of online knowledge as reference on their researches.

- Some of the online forums and blogs can be the potential places where predators can hunt their prey like your child. As children and teenagers, they often need to seek comfort and help from people outside from their families. In this way, they are open to any attacks.

- Pornography is rampant online. Some media sites contain this kid of materials such as images or footage. Not all multimedia contents are for knowledge gaining. There will be those who will try to harm the innocent mind of a child that he or she can be traumatized. These are too much for his or her understanding that could take the normal development of a child towards becoming an adult.

What are the Dangers Available Online?

Internet can be a place of library or market. There is a vast material which gives information that caters everyone who wanted to expound their learning.

The online has become the core place where the world entwined together with the sites where people can meet throughout the globe such as forums, blogs and the social networking sites. In this way, everyone gets the chance to voice out their opinions and certain emotions they are going through. Everyone now can post whatever thoughts he or she has online.

That is when the privacy of an individual is being violated. For those who are not aware, this becomes an open ticket for predators looking for potential prey. They feed on the thoughts and weaknesses of the victims. Once caught on their hands, you cannot get out anymore.

By this, internet has become the scariest place as of the moment. Credit card or bank account thieves are now rampant. Children molesters are also available now, predators who prey in the innocents of children.

There are also those websites that contain malicious contents. Once a victim clicks something, viruses are downloaded on their computer. They do not know that they have been a victim until they notice losing or corruption of files.

There are also sexual abusive person who acts as your friend at first and when the relationship will turn into the next level, the true purpose is revealed.

The internet is not a safe place anymore for your children. But parents can do something about the matter. Your children can still use the internet but with your own proper guidance and rules.

Danger in Chat Rooms and Social Sites

With a simple click on the mouse or few keystrokes, a child can know what is happening on their place or other places. This is because of the always new emerging technologies that enhance the communication of humans throughout the world.

This is how powerful internet is as of the moment. Unluckily, such power is equipped with danger for children or teenagers. As a child, they are fascinated in meeting new people and even talking with them in the internet using chat rooms or some social networking sites.

For adults, this new technology is not dangerous to them. But to children, especially if they are found out of their true age, it will be used against them for exploitation.

One of the most common child exploitation is in the chat rooms using sexual paraphernalia. The predator will stay on these chat rooms all senses are open, waiting for a child so innocent to talk to them. The most common issues are from girls who are more open and friendly toward making new friend. As soon as little girls start to share their inner thoughts, the predator will prepare them for the sexual activity.

The more the little girl is engaged to this predator, soon he will set up for an eye ball, means personal meeting each other. This will open to an invitation on the predator's place where the sexual activity can occur.

Children are very easy into believing about the true friendship happening virtually. But on reality, it's only an advance for someone looking for a victim. Because of this, a child will be too open and reveal information that should be private.

When this happen, the online thieves will be open to whatever he wish to do such as robbing the family, kidnapping and sexual activity. It can also be a way of your computer acquiring viruses, spywares or other malwares through the social networking sites and chat rooms. The viruses will eventually damage your computer.

Dealing viruses are very hard, especially if you are infected deeply. Often time anti-viruses are not enough to resolve the situation. There are those that needs formatting, it means losing all the important files stored in the computer.

There are no harm in social networking sites and chat rooms if you lecture your children to keep away from those evil people and links. A child who is expose in this kind of danger might lose the innocence he or she has. It will also affect the normal maturity of the child.

Once expose to pornography, the child will feel that there is a need to grow up fast.

But it is you, parents, who can stop this from happening. Keep your children from excessive use of social networking sites and chat rooms. Be prepared to fight for these things.

Danger in Online Thieves

Children, if not properly guide will give out personal information, this will cause an identity theft. What is identity theft? For parents who are not familiar with it, identity theft is someone who uses personal information without permission. This private information includes the credit card number, bank account information or social security number.

The thieves will use them for their own good. For example, if they extract the credit card information of a victim, they will go around online stores and shop. They can also try to withdraw money from the bank information they got. Soon, you will find out that mountain of money are already extracted in you or even leaving you debts that you will pay for.

Identity theft comes in different forms. They can be on spywares, in the form of phishing or hacking someone's website. As a parent, there is a need for you to protect your child's identity. No matter what age you are, the theft will not have second doubt in creating you a victim and get away with the fraud.

If any case the parents found out about their children giving information to a stranger, there are ways in which a parent can do to lessen the situation, if prevented early.

First, they can check and alert the credit bureaus to place a fraud alert on the credit report. In this way, the person has to be contact first before opening a new name. This is to prevent further damage. The important thing is to have a credit copy, in which a fraud alert is placed. So, parents can see for any discrepancies on the account that weren't made by you or your child.

Parents should also contact the companies where accounts have been opened and submit any related documents to support your claim. Never also forget contact the law enforcer. They will assist you with the matter and contact your creditor about what happened.

Danger of Spyware and Malware

Children browse different websites and click links that looks interested. Some are curious about downloaded things that are free like online games and video.

Children are not aware that those files may contain spywares or malwares. These kinds of programs are dangerous in your computer. If not prevented, you computer system will corrupt and crash.

Spyware is a tiny program that gets in your computer when you download a free program from the internet. It can be easily obtain from the too much clicking links or downloading files.

This program is very sneaky when invaded in your computer. It can determine how many keystrokes you are typing, what are the things you are typing and other stuffs that should be hidden and secure.

Another sneaky program is the malware, contains either viruses or spywares. Malwares duplicate themselves in your computer without you noticing.

Online thieves will be sneaky enough to create different websites that children might be interested. Once a malware is installed on those sites, it will retrieve the children's information and email address. Soon, spam emails are on their inbox.

What are the signs the Computer has Malwares?

- The computer is not working properly, prompt errors are showing and worst the performance is slowing down.

- The computer won't restart or shut down when you command it to.

- You open your browser and suddenly redirected to a website you did not want.

- You receive many pop-ads, even if you are not using the internet.

In case this happen, the first thing is to stop any online activity such as entering passwords or other private information. Install an internet security needed from your computer such as anti-virus and anti-spyware.

Make sure it is updated recently and conduct a regular scan in your computer. In this way, malwares, viruses and spywares are deleted on your system to stop further damage.

Parents also should be aware of the links and pop-up ads that suddenly appear on your emails and browser. They may contain malwares or spywares that will be downloaded on your computer if you are not careful on what you are clicking.

Never forget to lecture your child about the sites that offer free downloaded stuffs. Tell your children to ask for your help every time they want to download a video or game. Also, tell them not to enter user names and passwords to suspicious sites.

Downloading free stuffs can be sometimes tempting. But when downloading, it should be done on a safe and trusted website. Free stuff from a website is the often cause of all viruses, spywares and malwares. The child should be advice not to download such free stuff without you supervising.

Advice also your child not to click any links from the email they receive that are not familiar. They will just click links that they know who the senders are. If the child will accidentally click the link, be prepared that a malware, spyware or virus has been downloaded. Attachments on emails also contain these malicious programs.

Your children must be aware of how much cost it will be for repairing damage that malwares does. So in the future, your child will have second doubts on downloading files and other free stuffs.

Danger for Kids Falling into the Hands of Online Abductors

The rapid growth of cyber-crimes reported recently makes the internet as one of the scariest place to be. There will be worldwide predators lurking around to look for the next potential victims and your child might be the one.

Internet is an open medium for everyone to use and you cannot prevent your children from getting there. When your children are too lured from what they see and hear from the internet, they will be put on a danger mode. A lot of predators are looking for innocent children to become easy victims of their schemes.

Social circle in the internet are unlimited and the best place to meet people all around the world. In there, your child can meet someone they can think of as a friend material. They will feel as if they can be the friend whom they can trust and get comfort.

Due to this cyber-crimes such as online abduction become so popular and vastly growing over the internet. It is not new anymore of how many children have been kidnapped by people they just met in the internet.

At first, they will gain the trust and establish a so called "friendship" that they cannot have from others. Then, when everything becomes so intimate, they move to another level like meeting up in personal. This is when the abduction stated.

To prevent such matter, always tell your children on the scariest thing that people can do over the internet and the strategies that abductors are doing to lure your children. Monitor your children activities and the recent changes they are doing.

Why Your Child is the Potential Target Victim?

While our children are the greatest beneficiary of the internet technology, they also become the potential victims in the internet. While internet helps them from their education, it can also be the culprit of your child suddenly losing his innocent world.

So, why it is the child that predators become potential targets?

One of the traits of children is being impressionable that becomes their disadvantage. They easily give trust to someone who showed them goodness and kindness in any manner. This make goons prey for them such as asking private and personal information.

People like this are all over the internet with their very watchful eyes. This type of people maybe on forums, disguising as someone who can help them anything that your child needs. They can also be in chat rooms asking your child to be their close friends and slowly make the child comfortable with their sweet talks.

Children are easily lured to things they are not aware due to their explorative characters. Many will be lured to child's pornography; despite the effort of the governments all over the world still show no stopping. Predators will use pornography on children as their prey because of the innocence of the child and the craving to want and want information from the new discovery.

Children can be easily deceived, especially if someone will pose as their close relatives such as uncle or grandfather. Many online thieves will act as part of the family just to ask the credit card, bank account or other private information from the child's parents. Since a child thinks it his favorite uncle would give out the information easily without second doubts.

Internet is an exciting world for a child but can turn into the scariest place. Children will be the easiest victim from the cruel world of internet.

Signs that Your Child is in Danger

Often parents are not aware of their children sudden change of behavior. As parents, you should always monitor what your children are doing and the behavior they are portraying. If you suddenly see any changes, be alert and act quickly.

There will be many signs that your child is in the verge of danger with predators.

There is a sudden change of the closeness of your children to you. Your child will detach his self from the rest of the family. They become very cold towards family activities. Often do not eat with the family together that once they look forward.

You are not anymore the confidant whenever he has problems. Do not anymore talk to you unlike they used to. When they have been brainwashed by the predator, they put images on their mind which creates lies as barriers of the bond between you and your child.

You find that your child receiving gifts from someone you never heard of or not part of the friends he once invited in your home. This is another way that the predator will lure away your child from you and the rest of the family. The predator will send gifts as part of their so close friendship to get his or her trust.

Your child receives a plane ticket. Predator will use the so called build relationship and ask your child to have a meet up. Disguising that they are the only one who knows their interest.

When you enter their room, suddenly your child changes the website on their screen. It is a sign that they are looking something which is not supposed to be on their age. As you know you will be angry and will find all means to hide from you.

There will be changes of the accounts they previously use. This is for them to divert your attention when you are tracking their account. This is for them to access the predator's content without you noticing them.

Receiving massive phone calls from a person you never heard. When you try to ask them, they will just say that comes from a friend in school.

They will also detach their self from their friends. Since they have found someone who they think understand them well than the circle of friends he or she once have.

You find them spending too much time on the internet. You can see the problem when your child is spending late on the internet and too engross to be disturbed when they are supposed to be in bed.

Also, consistently staying on the comp
even on weekends. They spend too much t
on a forum or chat room site. If they are
home, all they did whole day was sitting
front of the computer which can be a perfe
day for predators.

These situations will not be good when you as
parents will not put guidance or control over
the situation. This can be very bad especially
when you are at work and your child is left at
home. He or she will have the freedom to do
whatever the predator asks.

If your child is not focus on the things that are
not right, he or she will be easily lure by these
predators that could damage the innocence
within. As you know that there will be many
who will offer nice and kindness to them just to
make them open.

When they are already open, slowly your child
will be away from you and is on the verge of
danger. If not stop immediately, you will find
yourself regretting you have never imposed
restriction towards the usage of internet.

As early as possible observe your child and if
you see any of these changes act immediately.
As a parent, you can do many things from all
those sort of dangers that internet offers.

As Parents: What Can I Do?

What can I do to stop my child from being a prey? The best thing to do is violate your child's right towards accessing the internet. You as the parents have all the right to guard and protect the child's interest and activities online.

It is your duty to protect your children from pornography and gambling that the internet can give. It is also your duty to keep the innocence of your child and grow normally.

This maybe a difficult task and eventually get you in the fight with your children. No matter what happen, you can explain to them that this is for their best.

Parents should not stop to monitor the websites that their children often visit. Continue monitoring on daily basis is what you can do to avoid them from being the prey.

Here are ways in which you can check your child's online activity:

- Chat rooms are the main places where a child can mix up with some sexual predator. Parents must monitor the emails that their child is receiving. There might be emails which contains a clue to what they are mostly doing online.

- Parents need to install caller ID on their phones. A caller ID will be useful for parents to know who are calling. If you think that it is the sex predator calling your children, you can ask the phone company to block the phone number.

- There is a law that no pornographic information should be passing to a child below 18 years old. As parents, you can report this to the service provider to track the service provider of the predator.

- You can also report such incidents to the local police or any country law enforcer. There are many who can work on this kind of cases such as tracking the predators IP address to know their locations. Make sure that you have the copy of evidences and the law enforcement can examine them.

- Parents can also install internet filtering software. This is to protect your child from browsing unwanted contents. The software will filter and block the sites that parents do not want to be seen.

- Make a copy of the conversation that is coming through between you and the children to know why they are hanging out with this kind of person. In this way, you will know why your child is getting away from you and is leaning on the stranger.

It is sad to know that there are growing victims of children in the internet from those online predators. Mostly are found on chat rooms that make it difficult to know who are true and who are wolfs that wait for the next victims.

Parents are the only one who can put stop to this kind of danger. There are many dangerous things that when parents find out, they will find all means to protect their children and monitor their online activities.

At first, you may feel guilty about invading your child's privacy but soon you will find that they are for the best. If you want to make your child safety, you will not want to get them involved from these schemes and scams. Parents can do many things.

Monitoring the child's online activities and installing internet filtering software are the best actions that parents can do. There are many children who are not engage in sexual relationships with some adults older than them. Through also the newest technology of protection, parents have been answered on the dilemmas going through the internet.

They are the responsible people to help their children and there are no one else can do it. If spying and snooping your children is the answer, soon enough they will see that it's for their own good.

Parents' Solutions for Online Danger

Parents can find many internet safety solutions for their children. This is thanks to the continuous growth of information technology towards fighting crimes in the internet.

All the chat rooms, forums and social networking websites make social life much wider through the connection in virtual reality. These social media can be used in good ways but we cannot avoid the fact that they also give bad effects, especially on children. Your child might be exposed to various dangers that as parents can be difficult to control.

You cannot really stop your children from using the internet since it becomes the latest trend. This is because children often see what adults do and they copy it from them. When they see what internet can do, there is no stopping them from using.

A solution to the constant exposure of your children is to regulate the access of the Internet. Monitoring of their activities online can lessen the danger they will be exposed.

Microsoft Windows allows you to create different account in which you can set parental controls for your child. The administrator side can limit the websites that a selected user to eliminate the danger. All it takes is some basic knowledge of parents from computer.

Another best solution is to install internet security in your computer. Each tie the child tries to access some pornographic sites or links, the software will automatically block them. This type of software is very easy to use and parents will never get difficulty.

Disallowing your children from using the internet is also depriving them from the technology of their generation. It is not a wise action. What you need is to educate your child before they can use the internet.

Training your child perhaps is the best way that you can do. Not only will your children benefit from this action but also you as their parents. You will have the chance to get close to your child and spend quality time for him or her. You can share some moments where you two can get a closer bond and lure him or her away from the danger of the internet.

Along with the boding, you can insert his or her responsibility when using the internet. Let him or her understand that he or she is not deprived from his or her right but everything has limits.

Let him understand he or she can use the social networking sites if only he or she will be careful from people whom she or he did not know. This kind of problem is mostly common to girls since they are vulnerable and much open of their selves.

Always make sure that you can be a friend of your little girl than the stranger they will meet online. Give the child the confidence to open up with you and you are there as their friend and not just parents.

There are many more solutions you can find as parents in solving the problem. Online activities can be educational to your children when there is a proper guidance from you.

Lecturing the Truth About Online

The best thing that parents can do is to activate the privacy setting of the computer to reinforce restriction usage of the child's activity on the internet. Then, check every social networking site to limit the things that you think are not good for them.

The most important thing is explain the rules and limitation you have set to your child. There are many things that parents should be lecturing to their children about online safety.

A child must be aware of the information they will post on the social networking site and how far it can reach. Also explain what is not good about it. Talk to them about strangers making them as potential victims who would talk about sexual contents that are not good.

Bullying can also be done online. There will be people who will spread not good and nasty information to hurt their feelings. Teach your child to not get involved in this kind of activity or else they will be the victim in the end.

If you cannot avoid the situation, your child will pay the consequence of being bullied online. Parents must be sensitive towards their children. If they sense that there is something wrong going through their child, they need to advice immediately before they seek refuge from others like the online predators.

If in case things are already out of place, ask for the authorities help. This is because they know what they can do in this kind of situation and can even tracked the culprit.

Lastly, make sure as a parent, you need to understand the private policies of the websites your child is visiting. In this way, you know the details of what the site can do if your child submits information. Parents have the right to review and remove the contents which they think will not be good.

Teaching Your Children the Truth about Internet

One way parents can make sure of the safety of their children from the internet net is teaching them about it. As we all know, internet is a powerful tool that is used in this modern world. It gives the convenient of looking for information without too much hassle with just a few keystrokes. Everything there is already in the internet and you all it need is to access the information. You can even access the information from miles and miles away news with only few clicks.

But internet can also give negative effects for those who misuse it. It is difficult for a child who is too much exposed in the internet. Many said that internet is a dangerous place. It is being where massive production of viruses that spread around the world.

Spywares are also the source of hacking as they invade the computer.

This is a place where you do not want your kids go snooping around. Internet is full of place that might be dangerous to them. As parents we need to teach them that wondering too much in the internet is not good. Because they are still small, they have to limit the areas they are exploring. You need to make them understand that this is for their own good.

Describe them the pros and cons that internet technology can bring. Show him the places that are not suitable for him and what danger could it bring. By teaching them, you are insuring the safety of your children towards harmful elements in the internet. Tell them it's not just for them but also for the protection of the family.

Tell your children that they should not be giving personal such as passwords and usernames to strangers that they know only through the internet.

Even if that person is very nice to them, tell them that they should not be fooled for the true intention.

The passwords are the predators aim to get what they want. If they get what they wanted, surely they will benefit from the information your child given. Soon you will find your credit card accounts fully loaded with bills you haven't even purchased.

Teach also your children about online bullying. These kinds of actions are not appropriate. If they do not want to be bullied, they should not also bully others. Tell them that using foul language is not also appropriate and that they keep their post clean. These things mostly happen because it is easier to respond foul messages to a person you haven't meet. What makes it dangerous is that the person your child is cursing might be an expert in the computer and danger the files.

You must also allow them to have fun but there are limitations. Giving them the total freedom to browse whatever they want will open them any predators lurking. As long as you explain to your children that what you are doing is for the best.

You must also never forget to tell your children not to accept any files without consulting you first. The file may contain viruses and spywares that could harm the important files stored in the computer.

Also tell them not to get close to strangers they only met online and try to befriend them. They are the predators that will only introduce his self as friend but as soon as he get the trust of your child will do his advance move.

Internet is now the most dangerous place as of the moment. A child can't combat the danger alone. As parents, you should be always prepared to combat with him and stay away from the danger.

Strategies for Parents to Avoid Their Children from Sexual Predators

The most common cyber-crimes that are being reported to law enforcement body are the fast growing of online sexual predators. They come from various age limits. Some maybe are adult and others are just a little older than your children. You cannot guess of who will be the predators of your children.

So, as parents we can do things to avoid our children from meeting these evil people. Here are the ways that you as parents can do for your child to lessen the chance of meeting sexual predators:

Parents should have time to teach your children online. Parents can enumerate and show your children what sites should they access regularly and avoid those might be the potential place where sexual predators are waiting.

Parents must always ask their children about what is going on around. Have time to sit and have a little chit chat to be. Make sure you make them feel that you are comfortable to talk with and you are there to understand not to condemn. You must also make them understand that what you are doing is for their best.

It is not good that you install computers in your children's bedroom. The computer should be always in the living room, where everyone can use and see what is going on.

If children will know that their parents can see what they are doing, they have less chance to go such dangerous sites.

Make sure that you have installed internet filtering software that can help block pornographic and gambling websites not suitable for your children.

Make sure that your internet service provider can also do the task. Just an added protection.

Tips for Children to Be Safe in A Social Networking Site

For years now, social networking sites have been the latest trends for children and teenagers. These sites included MySpace and Facebook that they often use to connect with other people and exchange personal information from each other. It becomes the most powerful tool in communication aside from chats. Social networking sites now are also equipped with chat box. That is why it has all that makes children and teenagers loved them.

Not only the amazing application of chat box but also they have the ability to share photos and videos that other people want to know about them. That is why children can be trapped in this kind of new technology and could put them to danger.

You may not believe but there are online people who are looking for children to be the next victim as young as 6 years old. Though some of these sites are not as popular like others such as Facebook or MySpace, but still parents should be always mindful about their children's activities online.

So, what can parents do to keep their children safe from these social networking sites?

Parents should always be aware of the activities of their children in the internet. Remember that children may not also use the computer but they can also use the cell phones to access the internet. As the parents, you should protect your children in all possible means. Even if it means blocking the internet access from the cell phone of your children, then better do it.

Children that are 6 and 7 that start schooling should be always watched over. In this ages are the crucial stage of being very curious. If parents are not watching, they surely do whatever they wish and see. Children with this age can be talk over and lectured how social networking sites can be dangerous.

Let them know that you are on the back watching what they are doing. But explain to them that you are not invading their privacy but just making sure that they are safe. You should also be mindful on what your children's activity in the sites and who are they talking. There might be many online predators disguising their selves in the social networking sites.

Parents should also remind their children not to post any personal information in the website. They should not post something that strangers can access such as usernames, telephone number, address and many more. The identity theft is becoming rampant and many people have already been victims. It is advisable to be mindful.

They must also be mindful on the pictures and videos your child is posting. Through this, the online predator can see them as potential victims and study your family background.

Remind your children also not to confirm any friend request that they do not know. Online predators will send friend requests to their potential victims and your child may get one.

Know What Kind of Emails Your Child is Receiving

Informing your children on some basic online safety is also as important as to teaching them the real security. Long ago, parents have taught us not to talk to strangers. This has been very useful now in the modern world of internet technology. As parents, you should be aware of all the possible means of ensuring the safety of your children every time they browse the internet.

One of the dangerous application is the email that parents should make their children not too much exposed and do not talk to strangers. Here are the things they might get in emails and the solutions to avoid them.

• Hazardous downloadable files that are attached in the emails. These files can contain viruses, spywares, worms and Trojans that will be a major threat in your computer. But you can install internet security software to detect and block the incoming threats. Some of the files will disguise itself from a looking harm less emails that your children might receive. Make sure that you tell your child not to click any of them even though they look innocent. Do not open especially if the sender is some unknown email. Much important than installing internet security is also making sure you have turned on your firewall. Never turn off the firewall because you will be putting your computer in danger.

- Your child will be exposed to verbal abuse. The person who are sending your children emails might contain inappropriate words that are not good on them. There will be many people who will send vicious, stupid and foil languages that might be the cause of verbal abuse to children. These include swearing or making sexual advances that contains in the email. Teach your children how to block emails containing such foul languages or sexual advances. Also, tell them not to contact anymore the person in the future. If the abuse is getting too much, as the law enforcement team to track and trace the location of the sender where you can file a case against child abuse.

- They can also be exposed to phishing. What is phishing? It is a kind of online scam using the emails. There will be people disguising as a close relative of your children asking about personal information from them. These people might also disguise as a bank representative asking to confirm something. Information they are getting usually involve credit card numbers, bank account information, home address, social security number and many more. The best defense you can have is by installing anti-phishing program in your computer to detect phishing links in the email or websites. This will directly avoid phishing your children. As we know that it is very easy to gain the trust of a child.

- They might receive an email that you do not want them to see such as links to pornographic sites or pictures of extreme violence. There are many websites uploaded in the internet that could damage the innocents from your child. The links can be sent through emails from a friend they acquire on social networking sites. To prevent this situation, parents can install internet filtering software that will allow them to block sites that contain harmful materials. You can also make sure that your child is protected always because of this software. Not only can you block the sites but also the links containing these harmful contents.

What is Monitoring and Protection Software?

As parents what we want is the best internet security protection because we want the safety not only for our computer but also to our small children. But managing this kind of task is not easy. You can find that many programs that claim the best internet protection for your computer. But only few of them will stand the best.

If you want to determine which program will do best, you can try some of them and see what suits you best. You can be the one who can examine it carefully to each pros and cons of the software. After that you can decide which software you will need, you are very comfortable with and easy to use. Do not also forget that you must sake software that will totally protect you one hundred percent.

There are a lot of internet security programs that will give a trial version fro few weeks or a month. This can help you parents to decide thoroughly what software to buy. Even if you are using the trial version, it is still good to know that you have some protection against the harmful agents.

Even also some internet service providers have their own protections that are preinstalled once you avail their service. It is the parents' decision if they want to activate the service offered by the ISP. The internet security will be automatically updated as long as you are connected to the internet. It is also important to download some optional updates when the announced it. The decision will be on the parents on how they are going to impose internet security for the safety of their children.

Whatever programs that you choose, it is very vital that you always update it to keep the security intact. Parents can also choose the updates and do it manually. But it is not necessary because they already have the functionality of automatic updates.

What you need to secure is the guaranteed protection of your chosen internet security that whatever happens your computer will be at no risk. The use of the protection is to filter the software running on your computer, the connection going through your network and the sites visited by your children. When your computer has this software, it is easy for parents to monitor their children.

As parents you have to weigh the pros and cons of the software you will be trying. In this, you will have an evaluation of what will be good not only to your computer, to your child but also to the entire family.

Here are the benefits that you should be getting from internet security software when choosing one:

1. The software must provide that your children cannot access unauthorized websites.
2. Have a good way of keeping your children from any sexual predators.
3. You can allow your children to browse the internet at minimal supervision because you feel safe by of the protection.

Here are the negative sides that your computer software might posses:

1. Parents may feel that it is not what they need and very hard to navigate or difficult to use.
2. Your child can easily see the loopholes of the software and still can break through the barrier. It will be useless because they can still see the sites which you forbid.
3. It only detects some malicious files and not guaranteed to have 100% detection.

What more is there About Child Safety Online?

As parents, to make sure that the activities of you children online can be the most fun thing without worrying about the danger. We have to set rules and boundaries regarding this activity to ensure the safety.

Let the child understand that giving out personal information to a stranger, even if he is very nice will put him on a danger and his family. All personal information should be kept in your young children so that they cannot give them to the strangers. In case they have found out it accidentally, make sure you brief him that it is not wise to be giving out information.

The computer should be in a place where it is open such as in the living room. This is because for you to be aware and see what activities he is doing online. Computer should not be put on a secluded area where he can sneak around and do whatever he wishes to do. Putting it on an open area makes the child doubt not to do whatever he wishes to do online.

Brief your child that if he observes something abnormal online, they should contact you immediately. Ask where they have found out the website and who are the people have given the links to them.

Parents must forbid their children in having a file sharing to a stranger they only met online. This will only make the online predator know the location of your house and can use for its advantage. The child will be more in danger for the situation.

As parents, you should know the accounts and passwords that your children are using. This is for you to access their accounts and see what activities they are doing and who are the person they mostly contacted. This is for you to monitor and whatever advances from a person you see, you can stop it immediately.

As parents, you should monitor the actions of your child. Prevent him from meeting this person in personal. You should let them understand that even though that person is nice but still they cannot know what the true motive is. This is because meeting up the person might put them on danger.

Be as a friend to your child and not just a parent. In this way, he or she will not hesitate to open up with you and less to inclining in looking for another person's comfort that they might find online.

Here are some ways you can do as parents. You are responsible for making them understand that what you are doing is for their best and not for their own good. Tell them that it's your way of showing your love to them and you do not want any harm befalls from them.

Tips for Children on their Online Activities

Here are some tips that parents can teach to their children about surfing the internet. This is to prevent them from getting into danger. If they can follow these tips, parents can be at ease that their children while online.

The child should obey their parents in putting personal information online that could make them potential targets. These include the address, phone number, bank account or credit card information.

The child should report any abnormal activities going on the social networking sites, email address or chat room to his parents. This is for parents to be aware and be alert with the situation.

The child should not give out username and passwords to a stranger. This is the biggest advance from your child.

The child should never accept gifts from strangers. If they have received something, they should send it back because they do not know the person.

The child should listen to his parents about the discussion of parents about safety online. The parents should set guidelines on a balance way in which kinds will not feel that they have been deprived from their rights.

The child should take it slowly knowing the person they only meet online. He or she must not give his or her trust easily. They did not even see the person so they do not know what to expect.

The child should not download photos from people who send them links.

About COOPA: Children Online Privacy Protection Act

What is this COOPA all about? In the year 1998, the Federal Trade Commission had established a law to protect the children against online. The law is what they called Children Online Privacy Protection Act or in short COOPA. This is a law that governs the child privacy while they are online to all website operators.

The website owners have these responsibilities following:

- Whatever personal information that they get from children such as name, email address and hobbies they are bound to protect the privacy.

- They are in need to explain what will be they doing about the information they have gathered from the children. Was it for marketing? Be used in announcing winners of a contest? Or give out the information in a chat room?

- The website operator should send notice if the information will be kept private or be forwarded to others.

These are the responsibilities that website operators should obtain from parents. They will not need this permission if only:

- Ask for a request from the child for only once.

- Notify the parent about certain things.

- Just to guarantee the child or website's safety.

- Give out newsletter or other updates about the website on regular basis to the email address of the child.

As website owners, they should ask parents about the information that the child enters on their website, just to check if they agree or not. Parents are allowed deny the request in any case they do not agree the terms of the site.

Conclusion

Parents are the model to make internet a safe place for their children. As early as possible, you have to act before it's too late. The longer you wait the more chance that your children will be in danger in the hands of online predators. This is an event that you as parents do not wish to happen.

Due to many children being so engrossed with the latest technology and much exposing their selves to the online threats and thieves, there is a bigger reason why parents should intervene the child's privacy in the internet.

It is not a joke that cyber-crimes are present in the internet. As a matter of fact, the number of victims is growing vastly. It is not a surprise anymore of how many children are reported of such certain crimes not only on your area but internationally. Many children, especially girls, are getting and getting curious about the world beyond their circle. They have been taking actions of wanting to grow up fast and leave the innocence of their childhood life.

Unfortunately, there are many who keep things secret from their parents afraid of being lectured or grounded. This makes it scary for parents that they are on the verge of being snatch away by someone they might not know. This is something that most parents would pray not to happen.

Many online predators will use the tool of internet to do their dirty businesses because they can disguise their selves. They will not be seen and even be hard to track. Some are even courageous enough to meet the child personality after being able to gain the trust. This is because internet is one of the greatest ways to communicate rapidly in real time.

If you are not going to pay attention to your children, soon you will find them in the hands of the cyber-crimes. You as a parent should acquire the knowledge and resources to prevent such things to occur. The consistency of your intervention should be always imposed for the rest of the childhood life of your kids.

Made in the USA
Lexington, KY
20 December 2012